A WRITER'S JOURNAL

Practical Journals and Diaries

FTL Publications
Minnetonka, Minnesota

Copyright © 2013 by Joan Marie Verba

FTL Publications
P O Box 1363
Minnetonka, MN 55345-0363
www.ftlpublications.com
mail@ftlpublications.com

ISBN 978-1-936881-18-5
All rights reserved.

Cover © Mega11 | Dreamstime.com

The author and publisher of this book assume no responsibility for the use or misuse of the contents, or for any physical or mental injury, damage, and/or financial loss sustained to persons or property as a result of using this book. The liability, negligence, use, misuse, or abuse of the implementation of any methods, strategies, instructions, or ideas contained in the material herein is the sole responsibility of the reader.

The material contained in this publication is provided for information purposes only.

The author and publisher have used their best efforts in preparing this book, and the information provided herein is provided "as is." The author and publisher make no representation or warranties with respect to the accuracy or completeness of the contents of this book and specifically disclaim any implied warranties of merchantability or fitness for any particular purpose and shall in no event be liable for any loss of profit or any other damages, including but not limited to special, incidental, consequential, or other damages.

A Writer's Journal

(Name)

This blank book may be used for:

- **a daily diary**
- **taking notes**
- **recording story ideas**
- **writing down your story or poem**
- **drawing or doodling**
- **keeping track of how many words are written each day on your current project (see end of journal)**

Project name   Project name

Date	# of Words	Date	# of Words

Notes:

www.ingramcontent.com/pod-product-compliance
Lightning Source LLC
Chambersburg PA
CBHW071217070526
44584CB00019B/3060